# The Windswept Verses

*poems by*

# Mark Kaplon

*Finishing Line Press*
Georgetown, Kentucky

# The Windswept Verses

Copyright © 2025 by Mark Kaplon
ISBN 979-8-89990-079-2 First Edition
All rights reserved under International and Pan-American Copyright Conventions. No part of this book may be reproduced in any manner whatsoever without written permission from the publisher, except in the case of brief quotations embodied in critical articles and reviews.

## ACKNOWLEDGMENTS

Special thanks to the editors of the following journals, in which some of these poems first appeared:

*Atlas Poetica, The Aurorean, Bear Creek Haiku, Canary, Contemporary Haibun Online, Fire Pearls 2, Four and Twenty Poetry, Frogpond, A Handful of Stones, Hawai'i Pacific Review, Hedgerow, Lilliput Review, Lynx, Ribbons, Tiny Seed Literary Journal, Three Line Poetry*

Publisher: Leah Huete de Maines
Editor: Christen Kincaid
Cover Art: Mark Kaplon
Author Photo: Mark Kaplon
Cover Design: Elizabeth Maines McCleavy

Order online: www.finishinglinepress.com
also available on amazon.com

Author inquiries and mail orders:
Finishing Line Press
PO Box 1626
Georgetown, Kentucky 40324
USA

# Contents

The Windswept Verses ............................................................................ 1

Dear Amnesiac, ..................................................................................... 22

*for Maui*

## The Windswept Verses

**1**

fluid and floating and nowhere

    whirlworlds unroll
warp bowl-like down and pull
stretched fabric to a vacuous intent
—jellylike, babies spill
from the shell, mud-caked
bottoms fracture into cells
and at nightfall stars
like bubbles to the surface arise
eyes crinkle at their edges
edges withdraw from sight
the wrinkles splintering into light


**2**

—windswept and wandering in a state meditative
    being blown around and, like the wind—penetrating….


**3**

*… in sunshine both space and time expand*

where was I? coming alive on my birthday
    breaking to pieces on the rainbow islands

and who is she? a girl today
    staying and straying on the rainbow islands

from a sunlit sea
see mountaintop to mountaintop arising
hear the crackle of rocks
in the bright light that falls

everywhere into place
forget your knees
to the breathlessness of peaks
and find them again by some pebbles

    … seize me, release me, leave me
everywhere in space to be dispersing…

and the colors of the wind parade
on the windswept way of the senses

crunching over the rough-country cliffs
a cold drizzle begins—
inhale huge drafts
of water in the air
sizzle to the sprinkling feeling
of drizzle on skin
watch the surf pour
to crevices it has worn, hold—
and back out the black rock pushing

    … whisk her, brisker, drop her
swifter over the crags like swift rains…


and the rainclouds and the fierce winds howl
after the raging of the waves

and to know every foot
of the land that holds you—
and, with soiled-brown hands,
set against the green of the land
and blue of the sky
sign the earth in gentle, rolling lines
loose with your tines
the living, pulsing root
of a carrot plant
bury the plants
in their beds to live

and bury me insensibly
over the earth from your open, rolling cart

lying on rock, drifting with the clouds
   —the only constant is constant change—
ripples of flame, patterns in the waves
   —paradise and creation are only sensations—
spearing reef-fish, inflating with the stars
   —and heaven and earth forever simultaneous!


and the wheeling colors celebrate
on their way without a destination

wandering islands roam until they die—
with footsteps wrapt and dwelling
           in whatever kind of weather
we live our lives with the space to be free
find in our eyes horizons on horizons



4

frigid night wind
         a boy blowing with abandon
                   the covered night

branches are black on the pond in winter
         a wanderer's—let those be my clothes

where no stars are
         no sky, nothing to hold
                   nor dim outlines

only the first desireless rain
         falling all night through bare stone

the broken-hearted knew
         a hole in their hearts

—sorrow is not despair—

homelessness is the greatest despair
    for the homeless have as ghosts become

(wrapped up in scarves
    even the nearest trunks
        seemed far away)

on the brink of blackwater bluffs
    a silhouette is breathing its own cold breath

and when your very
    world itself has been cast
        into floating disarray

on cold wind stripping away to bones
    the windblown horizonless black


5

strange dawn light
I wake to strange eaves—
now whose life is this?


6

Although you are
one ocean
and seven generations
away, today,

wandering poet
the air is in the mountains
in clouds, across space,
skies, the day-moon—its mountains—

and I leaving a trail
of your pocket poems chant
the poems of our boot-soles—still going—
and our soles are home


7

Getting lost
the narrow foot-
trail snaking
in and out
of I'ao stream to the back
of I'ao valley
I crossed
over moss and thickets
when sinuous
waters sped
in the diminishing dusk
a hard load
strained my breathing
rushing blood
pained my ears
when I set my pack
on a warm brown patch I'd found
just ahead though the way
was wrapped in a tone-
from-behind
that shone
almost like a sound
I couldn't keep up
and found myself standing
in the floating hand
of a citrus grove
a long time abandoned
with one hung fruit
incandescent in the dusk
and sat down to eat
in the grove right
where my hands found me

**8**

Hung stone
slants
over pools the sponge
mosses grow
in the cold
older than seasons

it is for those living generations
upon generations away
and the reflection I see there

it is for your love and approval
I pause to scribble these ripples


**9**

In a sugar-green valley I will wake
to glassy panes that seal the sky
ridges of jagged teeth will teeter in the sea
and in the east one vaporous peak reside
cloud-fleets will ring the horizon: radiating light
and in their center a vital-green island will rise
my companions'll ask: how many days ago we came
and I will only say: I think I've been here always


**10**

In the center of farm fields, standing
       the land around growing
              emerald translucent green,
      the sky a pearl of light blue
        where close white masses of clouds hang...
the good earth beneath me;
        the gaseous, spacious fluid dome above me—
the obsessive, heartbreaking beauty of the BLUE and white,

GREEN and brown—the indescribable brown soil of sunset—
of this moment I am on—in, with—a *planet*! the EARTH!

## 11

I dream of golden setting suns and a great
    rolling-of-the-earth
with gourds and ceremonies, and painted bodies everywhere,
    and everywhere remembering
who they are, where they are, where they come from

at the foot of towering, wild-snowy peaks
    breathed upon
    by blustery salt-winds,
ample and abundant, slopes of the potatoes spread—
the hunter-farmers of the heights plunge
    their arms deep
    into wounds of earth
and pull out, pumping, these organs of the earth's mantle

across the rain-gauze and the drift
    of drift-blown grasses
the head of an errant pheasant remains—
the hunters of the plains trailing,
    shifting, are fixing
in their zig-zag sights the frame of the bird—
an antenna of lightning connecting earth and sky

atop a rock, perched, in blackwater shallows
    a planter-fisher of the narrows
    gazes, in the same motion
as the carp moving—in the same current coursing
    and with pointed spear strikes
    into flesh, in the brown-green
of the clear stream twirling, in the brown-green swirling

and like a field of falling boulders
    here and there where they are

          and perfectly into place
the nomads are on the go—gallop-swimming,
            riding downwards the mountain,
with each foot firmly rooted in the empty-flowing sands
            with pots, kettles, tattooed skins
            and footprints that vanish
as breath in the shadow of far-blue, vaporous peaks

and to give in to hunger, exhausted and alone,
          on the fringes of an old mountain forest—
peering into the dim forms and the darkness
            catch visions of bright orange and ancient men
            in spaces circling a campfire... together resting,
              gaining... the weathered-leather of their hides—
and to realize as ceremony the meal

... to travel far is really just remembering....


## 12

Upon these ocean-cliffs which stagger in and out into the distance
            bursts of white mist leap against black rock
              lighting up the cliff-line...
far away in the calm blue dark, huge waves form, and lunge
          lunging on and on in one giant line toward the cliffs, crash—
klp'lsshhh—
        and break
                into a myriad white specks shooting high in the air
                  shrouding the far coast in massive clouds of vapor
        then pour
                in a thousand thin and thick waterfalls
                down crevices in the cliff wall
returning back to the wide-flowing waves of the great ocean
of rises and falls... pulsating... with crests merging, splashing,
the whole moving as one fluid motion....

**13**

Blowing fiercely my clothes
and hair the wind
in the way of the waves—
swept up, like a wave, in the winds


**14**

Gold-bronze orb of the moon arcs down
    beyond the dome of earth, its bright close light vanishing…
    the Universe explodes into sight—
  trillions of brilliant fiery stars illuminating forever in space
    above and below the plane of earth…
outwardly expanding spirals
    of black wind ribbon, sparking and extinguishing,
    and points of light join in planes, pores of light pour visions…
see galaxies away, and feel now the surging
    through the stars into the far fiery reaches of black space
    that is to ripples and splashes and threads diminishing
    that is surrounding and surrounding forever into infinity.…


**15**

Words wander out
by breath to the edge of the sky
where, with time enough
alone, they range over and there—and
fledglings no more
migrate finally back to fall
effortless, into place


**16**

Footsore and scrambling

over the shards and slabs labyrinthine
                of the jagged, stagger-rock sea-cliffs
a twist in the crags, skin-snagging, grabbed me
        and left them for shreds my boot-heels unraveling
I leapt, with shoulder-straps, a pebbled basin and passed
        over coves and the caverns concave
                where crashing waters dashed in in twists
                    the crumb-rock crumbled in my eyes like landslides
                and the clouds, massy and floating for no one,
                        emptied themselves out
                            to a useless-blue ocean
spirals, holes, a crescent to begin with—
carved in the rock: lightning and turtles, puffed sails
    and swelling torsos sitting in power—
across weather and the generations
        some wayfaring people part the air between us


## 17

Awash the drowsy
malaise of my eyelids
on a cloudy afternoon—

I wake up to solid rock,
wild rock, the shock of the real


## 18

*on a broke black branch*
*snagging my shoulder strap—*
*goddamnit*

Inside the walls of the tent I sit stinking—
my clothes now stained with sweat.

Even faintest sun presses on my sores;
my hair is matted and thick like bristles.

I'm tired, yawning, and it's only early afternoon.
My muscles ache on the dirt.

You say I should come to where you are,
but terns have found the ocean large enough for their feet.

I haven't missed a thing


**19**

a cluster of flame, a candle
on the yawning, cavernous dark—
this town in the hills


**20**

Rolling gently and foldingly down to the sea
        a far green country: a far rolling—in that dabbed
            and grassy feeling—
        a bright-green hill country...
around a bend in the road full-throated
        birds from their hollows peaceably sing
while broad-legged trees, shaggy and leafy and heartily growing,
        in shapes of ripe fruit fulfill the hillsides:
I lie in their shade and drink nourishment through my eyelids...

planting festival—
spinning out their ruffled skirts
our marigold women

carrying and in waves up the slopes
        the fragrant breezes flower
            through the grasses, rustling the grasses...
waters of the bay sparkle
        in easy, sailing crests... sparkle and toss...
... the bounty fleets... spun from down...
and showering over all's the sky—a baby blanket blue—

        radiant sunlight pouring dark leafy boughs….

lifting the brim
of her hat swelling over
bold-blue youthful eyes—
suddenly the air
was floating in marigolds

a far rolling, bright green place… dotted in spots with horses
    and cows… gourds, tossing—
        and the green translucent grasses blowing and twirling
            in the wind at my feet
        are to my eyes shocking and captivating and as marvelous
        as the broad landscape after having watched it awhile

pangs of the past can pass me, but can't hurt me…
    beneath breathing canopies—I feast my eyes
    … peace, green, and happiness….

## 21

infant fingers spin
and spin again its mama's hair
drinking on her breast—

wings folding, moon moth,
now, spasms on a flower

## 22

*meeting a child in hilltop fog—*
*greeting the brief sunrise of her smile*

This village in the clouds
with its lanes and little gardens
its kitchens and wood cook stoves
that make for us for lunch a soup bowl

of chunked bread and hard vegetable greens
and leave their residue on our spirits
like early morning wistfulness or the trees in mist.
By herself in middle age a mother
tours the rear of the houses
that slosh up and bank on adjoining slopes
and follow in the footsteps of the children.
I followed around
in the warmth of her attention
like somebody depending on a partner
to pick a trail through crags,
and even though we didn't
have a name for each other, her temper
drizzled lightly on me all afternoon
in the lightly drizzling midst of the village.

## 23

*arcing the glade a hummingbird plunges*
  *and arrives*
*precisely at its flower*

Tucked away on the mountainside: I flitter for days

       when night was late
and transpiring the skin of the tent

    the air came, like raised hairs, to rest on my face

    and with a noise here and there

and changes in the air—
    waking intermittent as rain all until dawn

        … until

far and resounding, near and surrounding—
    bird-symphony in the forest

  forcing me awake: I undo the tent-cloth
    gray-blue, sober dawn in the woods

   so sober and real and awakening

and all across logs and the leaf-litter
    sunrise pours
   colors from deep in the hearts of things

having slept and woke in this wood more than once
   to leave would be like leaving living

     but in thickets
  can spiders spin away from their webs?

white fog creeps through the trees
  breathing eucalyptus in my nose

and with the scents of leaves and who-knows to delight you

smelling the scent of strawberry in a eucalyptus forest
   where there are no strawberries to be found


## 24

Seas of gold juices suffuse
and overwhelm the afternoon—
herds follow home the mountain road…
purple and indistinct
distant peaks dissolve
dry tan grasses blur
to mist and the shadows
of rocks drag like momentum behind

    in the static of the hour
   the stasis of the sundown
  in the fleetingness of the moment

      that makes somehow
      such an eternity of the moment

as breath and the track
of my footsteps hang suspended
I'll walk once forever in the sound
and the silence of the sunlight


## 25

How *could* I deny it? I am in love
      with this place— the rolling upcountry…
in love my footsteps returning to the soft,
      moist, slumbering-brown soil of the field
the green clusters of leafy weeds
      growing in the edges. All the vegetables—
      flame-fringed carrots, cool water-flesh cucumbers,
          hearty and homey potatoes, the unruly tomatoes!,
      and tall beans awkwardly-leaning—
all buried in healthy brown dirt…

The spacious sloping hills of dry tan grasses and bushes
the green vibrant wall of corn stalks, the brilliant blue sky
      and golden sunset illuminating all in dramatic gold beauty…
in love I awake to the rooster, sprinkle cool, sweet, refreshing water
      over the herbs, wash dirt from the roots, watch the chickens
          roam about, the goats and pigs, the dirty barn!…
the quaintness of the entire country, of modest wood houses
      dotting the hills and fields, the quiet of the dusk,
      the darkness of the night… mad I am mad for it all…
cooking potatoes and chickens in the barn stove,
swishing pouring water over the bowls, spotting the little birds,
      nesting, flying, chirping…

    The orchards! citrus trees, apple trees, orange!
    The little white shed and wheelbarrow, gleaming in sunset!
    The stacks of firewood, chopped and kindled!
    The heap on heap of compost, buoyant in late afternoon light!

The vast purple and pink clouds of twilight!

Let me in love be laid amongst these rolling folds of hills,
    dotted in beddings, and surrounded by forest, mountain
    and rivers forever in all directions—
  insignificant and free beneath the far-spreading sky!


**26**

Morning after the storm—
I carry the watering buckets
to water the horses—carry
buckets of rainclouds in my hands


**27**

To get in contact with heat and wind
and leaves buzzing on the trees
I sit cross-legged on the dirt
and drink hot coffee from my cup.
I love my sunburnt arms and neck
the birds and chickens talking
and hope for a little tobacco to roll.
If everything rots where it drops
and weeds leaf out to their own design
why should I be modest or adored?

**28**

...swing... drive...
pick-axe into bare hill-side
swing... drive... swing...
to dig a hole to put a tree
drive... swing... drive—

the air is nice
thoughts float light....


**29**

With the light of the late afternoon
      shattering into sprinkles
            after a long dry day
to carry the watering can to the herbs, full of water,
      and spray in crystal-lit-up cool mist
         greening and glistening and vitalizing my plants
      the cool moist mist...
and to breathe the air full of water, the smell of water,
      and the touch of my hands in the light mist
      slowly opening, with the cracks all freed
         and dripping
    with crust of the fields....


**30**

Shirtless, shiftless, I think of you
drifter on the beach who is so much like me
combing the sands looking for footprints.
You left your skin snagged somewhere
to ebb and dash among the crags
and hid yourself away in plain sight.
But I have given up my nook in a thicket
for a pair of tines and the daily routine.
Send me some news of you:

are you there still walking the golden
sands on the beach of last week's sunset?


**31**

Fetching eggs for supper—

    crowded along the edge of their coop
        the chickens
    all facing
    across the valley
    toward the setting sun


**32**

Stay awhile with me
    by the wash basin—

while the pouring water swishes
    over the bowls
and the strain
of that all-day sun
drains down the bottoms of our feet


**33**

    When we get to that age
it'll be a long and late afternoon
with white onions glistening in oil
and empty light on the rafters.
There'll be potatoes on hold in the oven
airy heaps of basil rinsed and ready
and the laughter will long since have died on the bell
where people have left the place
vacant in the warm sun. You'll be there

with sun-washed eyes, bright and transparent
from the day's work
where you knelt in the beds
and worked in fresh compost.
And like this, with our bellies full
and a bunch mellowing on the beam
you and I—we'll die in our beds.


**34**

I sat thinking in the scattering dusk
of distant coasts and the meetings there
until setting my feet I found myself
      in a world of starlight—
the sky'd fallen, all dewy, into grass


**35**

The farmer bends his gaze all day
on the dirt, sleeps all night

in his bed, and wakes with time to the gentle
rolling rows of his land that stretch

like a signature before the window.

He makes his living by making the bull
pull his plow, the weeds conform to his plan

and turns in late afternoon sun to see
his shadow emblazoned by the watering can.

But skinny bulbs are hardier than fat ones
and caught chickens new, since birth, to feeding time.

When the dying fire of day flames up
on the clouds above

I'll plunge my body into water
and bathe off the itch of these fields.


**36**

All week long
        been weeding this field plot, planting the bean crop.
It is a shame for me
        that I can't keep from watching those moths
        who hover, past the rows in the goldenrods
        landing in, drinking, and billowing off again
        in the direction of cloud-torn, vaporous cliffs....


**37**

Unseen the wind starts in the leaves
        and her hand now
is nowhere in the dark

tomorrow I am leaving

        already the stars warp out
to some other sky away south


**38**

Not expecting to stay
the wanderer is everywhere seeking death

so fleetingly he feels
things and things
and stays in feeling
with the fleeing of things

in thin, gleaming branches he sees
summer spider webs

in ancient tracings remembers
what those hands knew

in solitude, dreams of her


**39**

Walking in a going gust of air—
    and to know the windswept way of the soul….


**40**

when failure and death and further instructions
    finally are forgotten from your senses

when miles are to go, the stones begin to glow,
    and you've for sustenance only breath

when finally exposure takes you, naked and exhaling,
    and knowing is a feeling almost physical

listen… the whole world is speaking—can you hear
    those trees, these poems, the sun's light, the quiet?

**Dear Amnesiac,**

        Yes, your pyramids were raised
Roughly up at right angles
To exert out loud and bright in the jungle
And obscure in darkness the jungle around—
And how many years is it you're living
In fear of the darkness there created?
You've your back to the door and the four corners
You're standing in a room with walls and a floor
But just the same as any other
You've stood in in pictures or places before.
Alien in your place of birth, you pound
An outraged fist into your palm, but are
Too over-tired and too much adrift,
Not at home, grown absent in an absent world.
So—your steam engine roared
Across space and the four seasons,
And from conductors' hands unloaded
Its surplus even to the farthest hamlet.
Yes, your transportations have taken you
Beyond the known horizon, but not any
Nearer to infinity, nor to eternity.
That is the moon double-paned in the window-glass
But could just as well be another bulb reflected.
Afloat, nowhere, a ghost you have become
You having from many hands vanished.
Your mind will not stop wandering, and all over
These carnival streets is too much noise for hearing.
You have withdrawn from this; are living in fear.
You fear death and the chances of death
So far removed you live from dying...
And waking up you find the day is there,
Existing, all-ready, you can only enter—
And looking to the night you see a frontier that's
Cold, empty, like it's a world you've never known.

Too furious for the ruin of your world.
But every thing in ruin must first be made—
A wildfire only burns, transforms
The wood, and passes. It is not a collapse.
Too anxious you're striving to build a new day:
Every morning only awaits your being born.

**MARK KAPLON** teaches literature and Hawaiian culture on the Big Island of Hawai'i. He began writing poems in earnest at age 18 after witnessing the sunrise from the summit of Haleakalā, or the House of the Sun, Maui's great peak. His poems can be found in dozens of journals: *The Aurorean, Hawai'i Pacific Review, Frogpond, Lilliput Review,* and *Tiny Seed Literary Journa*l among them. This is his second chapbook. His first, *Song of Rainswept Sand*, was written for his wife Hannah and published in 2014 by Finishing Line Press. After a ten year hiatus, he began writing again in 2024 following the birth of their first daughter, 'Iliahi Rose. Follow his work on *The Wandering Poet Cafe* and *Eat And Be Eaten HAWAI'I* social media channels.

www.ingramcontent.com/pod-product-compliance
Lightning Source LLC
Chambersburg PA
CBHW022103080426
42734CB00009B/1471